Write your name.

The sink is blocked. When the water runs away it makes a glugging, gurgling sound, *g, g, g.*

G g

Action: Spiral your hand down, as if water is gurgling down a drain, and say, *g, g, g, g.*

glug glug

glug glug

g g g g g g g g g

g g g g g g g g

g g g g g g g

plu_

_ift

fro_

G Capital

G G G G

Inky finds a switch near the bookshelf. She presses it a few times to see what happens. The light goes on and off, *o, o; o, o; o, o.*

O o

Action: Pretend to turn a light switch on and off, and say, *o, o; o, o.*

on off on off

on off on off

O

o

o

Capital

O

_ctopus

r_·bin

s_·ck

O

5

Bee has a new umbrella. She puts it up in the rain – *u, u, u, up, umbrella!*

U u

Action: Keep one hand steady and raise the other, as if putting up an umbrella, and say, *u, u, u, u.*

up umbrella

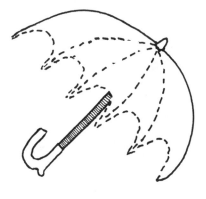

up umbrella

u u u u u u u u u u u

u u u u u u u u u u u

u u u u u u u

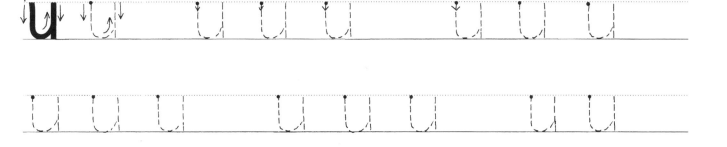

Capital

_p

s_n

dr__m

U U U U

7

L l

Snake is licking a lovely lemon lollipop, *llllllllll.*

Action: Pretend to lick a lollipop, saying, *llllllllll.*

lick a lollipop

lick a lollipop

_emon

umbre__a

hi__

Capital

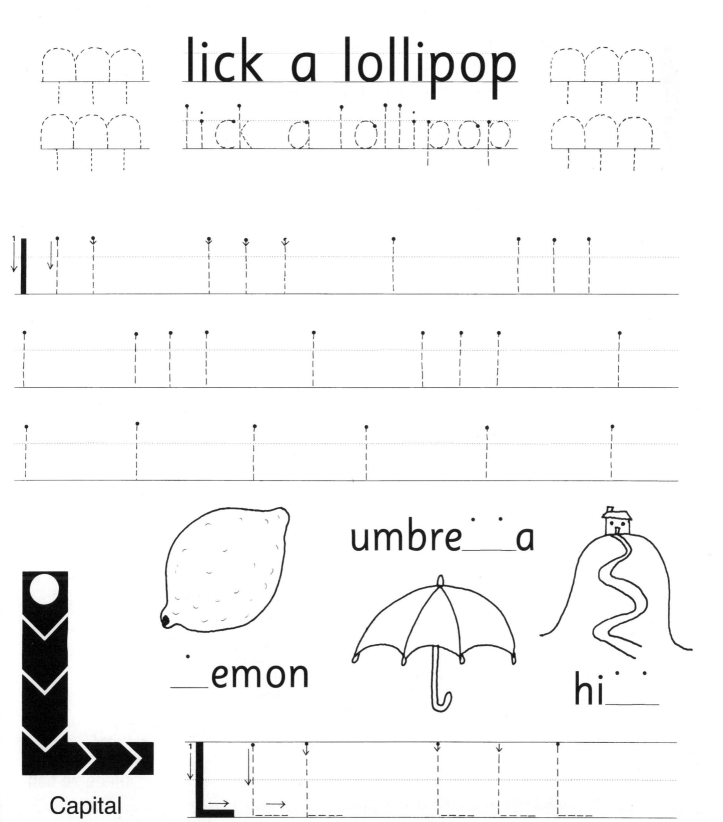

F f

Snake tries to catch an inflatable fish as it floats by. There is a strange *ffffff* sound and the fish goes flat. Snake's sharp fangs have punctured the fish!

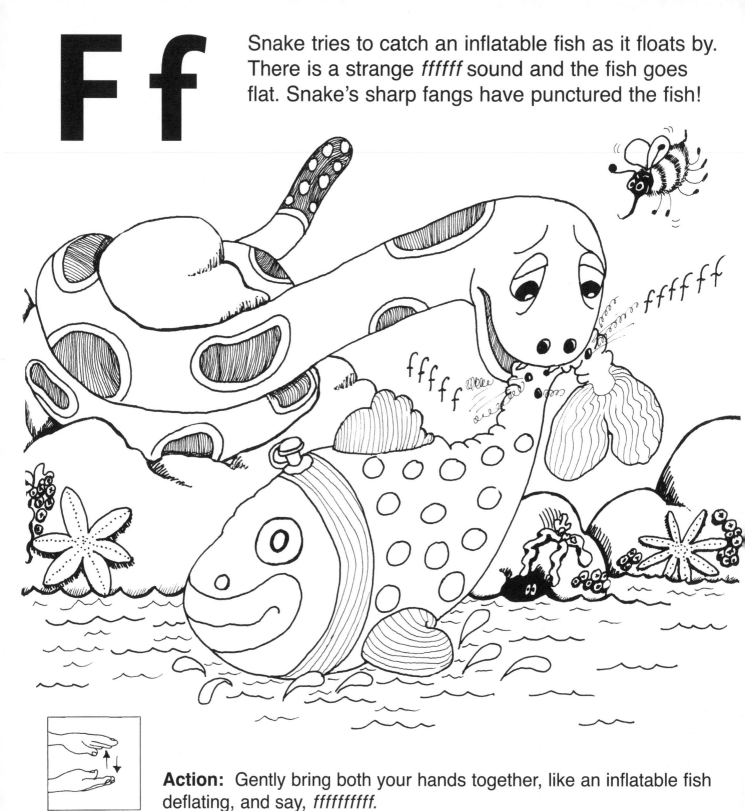

Action: Gently bring both your hands together, like an inflatable fish deflating, and say, *ffffffffff.*

flat fish

flat fish

f f f f f f f f f

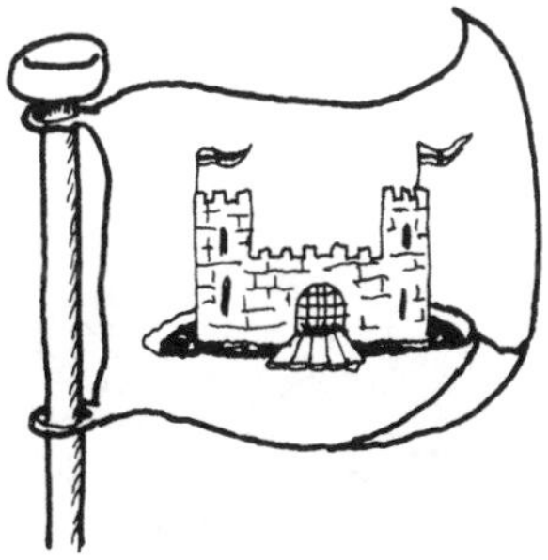

f f f f f f f

f f f f f f f

_lag

_rog

o_

Capital

F

Inky, Snake, and Bee are playing in the park. They hit the ball with a bat, *b, b, b.*

B b

Action: Pretend to hit a ball with a bat, saying, *b, b, b, b.*

bat and ball

bat and ball

b b b b b b b b b

b b b b b b b b b

b b b b b b

ra___it

_i_

cra_

Capital

B B B B B B

Some words are tricky and have to be learned.
Here is one way to help you remember them.

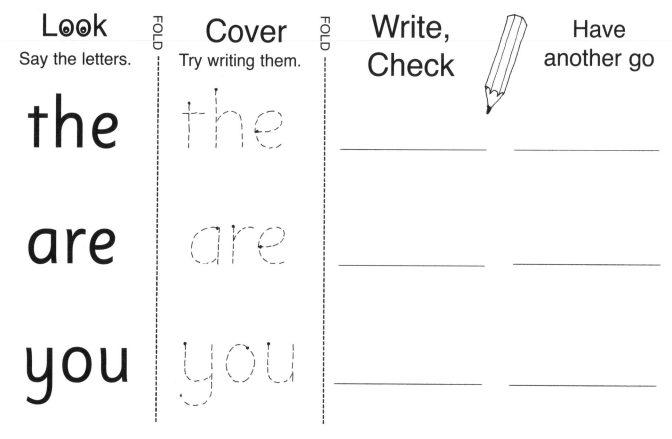

Look	FOLD	Cover	FOLD	Write, Check	Have another go
Say the letters.		Try writing them.			
the		the		_____	_____
are		are		_____	_____
you		you		_____	_____

Write in the missing letters.

the   ar_   y_u

a_e   t_e   _re

yo_   th_   _ou

14

Match the small letters to the capitals.

Practice the ‹o› shape, and put
the spots on the snakes.

Do you know these sounds? Trace over the dotted lines, then draw a picture of something that begins with each sound.

a	h	l
i	r	u
s	c k	f
n	d	o
i	e	b
p	m	g

How quickly can you say the sounds?

Write in the missing sound for each word.

b _ g   h _ n   b _ s

d _ g   c _ p   p _ g

m _ g   p _ n   s _ n

Read the words in the logs. Match each word to the picture in the frog that rhymes with it.

fun

red

mat

big

grab

log

When two letters that make the same sound come together, you only say the sound once: /r-a-bb-i-t/.

Read each word and draw a picture of it in the space.

rabbit

kitten

dress

hill

duck

parrot

Choose the right word for each picture and write it underneath.

met   mat   man

m a t

log   dig   dog

_ _ _

cup   cut   cap

_ _ _

peg   egg   pig

_ _ _

net   nut   not

_ _ _

and   ant   act

_ _ _

hen   hat   pen

_ _ _

bin   bus   bug

_ _ _

sob   sit   sun

_ _ _

Can you hear the sounds in these words? Write them down in the right order and read the word. Then draw a picture of each word.

hat	pen	ant
ink	man	cap
bed	dog	bus

Numbers need correct formation, just as letters do.
Trace over the dotted lines to write the number 3.

1   2   3

Count the caterpillars.

3 3 3 3 3 3 3

Find the 3 caterpillars.

three three three

Activity

Flat-fish race

Cut a fish shape from a piece of newspaper. Fold another piece of paper into a concertina, and use it to fan your fish along.

Make a mobile

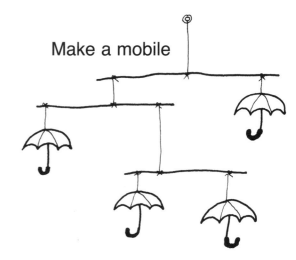

Cut some umbrella shapes from card. Decorate them and hang them as a mobile.

Lemon ice cubes

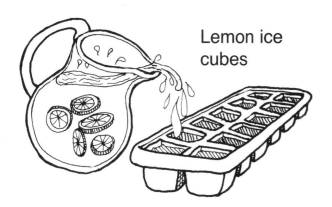

Make some lemon ice cubes from a lemon drink poured into an ice cube mold.

Read a story

Read the story of *The Three Billy Goats Gruff.*